MW01225987

English Writing Exercises for Second Language Learners: An English Grammar Workbook for ESL Essay Writing (Book II)

by

Stephen E. Dew

© 2015 hbicambodia.com

All rights reserved. First Edition

License Notes:

Table of Contents

1.   Preface

I wrote this second workbook for my academic English writing classes. It contains questions and answers on topics associated to developing good English writing skills. The second English writing exercises book has more topics associated to improving your academic English writing skills. The questions are typical of those asked in exams for an English diploma for university entrance.

These additional exercises are practical exercises to help support my previous three *"Academic Writing Skills"* series books:

- *"Learn English Paragraph Writing Skills - Paragraph essentials for ESL Students"*
- *"Practical Academic Essay Writing Skills - Essay essentials for ESL Students"*
- *"The 5 Step Essay Writing Process - English Essay Writing Skills for ESL Students"*

The 20 exercise groups with more than 200 questions cover grammar areas required for fluent and confident academic English writing skills. They include:

- General theory
- Sentence errors: Fragments, Run ons, and Comma splices
- Capitalization Commas
- Sentence combining
- Appositives
- Sentence Structure: Simple, Compound, and Complex
- Subject / Verb agreement

As well as the common grammar questions, I have included questions to aid in developing paragraph and essay writing skills.

These include:

- Topic sentences
- Supporting sentences
- Quotations
- Paragraph Unity
- Paragraph Coherence
- Prepositional phrases
- Some example of transition signals.

I would recommend ESL Students in low-intermediate to low-advanced English classes use this workbook for developing their academic English writing skills. As I said in my last book, "Academic essay writing is an essential skill for universities, colleges, and other tertiary educational institutions. Moreover, English writing skills form a part of the assessment requirements of many courses at university, college, or even high school." Thus, I believe it is extremely important you can do all these various kinds of English grammar exercises to become a competent academic English writer.

I sincerely hope you find some value in answering a combination of multiple choice and written questions. The best part is you get immediate feedback whether you are right or wrong through the answer key. The whole idea is to help you learn more, as well as, have fun learning.

Best of Luck,
Stephen E. Dew.
Author and TESOL Instructor.

2.   Capitals

Choose the correct answer.

1. the pastor of the church on market street is father murphy.

 a) The pastor of the Church on market street is father murphy.
 b) The pastor of the Church on Market Street is father Murphy.
 c) The pastor of the church on Market street is Father Murphy.
 d) The pastor of the church on Market Street is Father Murphy.

2. my uncle sambat told me many stories about fishing along the banks of the mekong in Cambodia.

 a) My Uncle Sambat told me many stories about fishing along the banks of the Mekong in cambodia.
 b) My Uncle Sambat told me many stories about fishing along the banks of the Mekong in Cambodia.
 c) My Uncle Sambat told me many stories about fishing along the banks of the mekong in Cambodia.
 d) My uncle sambat told me many stories about fishing along the banks of the Mekong in Cambodia.

3. one of the courses required for a ba in physics is statistics 302.

 a) One of the courses required for a ba in physics is Statistics 302.
 b) One of the courses required for a BA in physics is statistics 302.
 c) One of the courses required for a BA in Physics is Statistics 302.

d) One of the courses required for a BA in physics is Statistics 302.

4. phnom penh is the capital of cambodia in southern Kampuchea and is located on the mekong river.

a) Phnom Penh is the capital of Cambodia in Southern Kampuchea and is located on the Mekong River.
b) Phnom Penh is the capital of Cambodia in southern Kampuchea and is located on the Mekong River.
c) Phnom Penh is the capital of Cambodia in Southern Kampuchea and is located on the mekong river.
d) Phnom Penh is the Capital of Cambodia in Southern Kampuchea and is located on the Mekong River.

5. sivlong heng, a recent graduate of the royal university of phnom penh, is the cambodian video-gamer champion known as kiko.

a) Sivlong Heng, a recent graduate of the royal university of Phnom Penh, is the Cambodian video-gamer champion known as Kiko.
b) Sivlong Heng, a recent graduate of The Royal University of Phnom Penh, is the Cambodian video-gamer champion known as kiko.
c) Sivlong Heng, a recent graduate of The Royal University of Phnom Penh, is the Cambodian video-gamer champion known as Kiko.
d) Sivlong Heng, a recent graduate of the royal university of Phnom Penh, is the cambodian video-gamer champion known as kiko.

6. candidates for the position with the mining company must speak the english language as well as khmer.

a) Candidates for the position with the mining company must

speak the English language as well as Khmer.
b) Candidates for the position with the Mining Company must speak the English language as well as Khmer.
c) Candidates for the position with the mining company must speak the English Language as well as Khmer.
d) Candidates for the position with the mining company must speak the english language as well as khmer.

7. one of the most important cambodian holidays is khmer new year, which is in the fourth month of the chinese calendar.

a) One of the most important cambodian holidays is Khmer New Year, which is in the fourth month of the Chinese calendar.
b) One of the most important Cambodian holidays is Khmer New Year, which is in the fourth month of the Chinese calendar.
c) One of the most important Cambodian holidays is khmer new year, which is in the fourth month of the Chinese calendar.
d) One of the most important Cambodian holidays is Khmer New Year, which is in the fourth month of the chinese calendar.

8. in the opening lines of the poem, the man from snowy river, the poet, a. b. patterson, gives his inspirational description of australian outback.

a) In the opening lines of the poem, The Man from Snowy River, the poet, A. B. Patterson, gives his inspirational description of australian outback.
b) In the opening lines of the poem, the man from snowy river, the poet, A. B. Patterson, gives his inspirational description of Australian outback.
c) In the opening lines of the poem, The Man from Snowy River, the poet, a. b. patterson, gives his inspirational

description of Australian outback.

d) In the opening lines of the poem, The Man from Snowy River, the poet, A. B. Patterson, gives his inspirational description of Australian outback.

9. my uncle john taught his parrot to sing the words from the old rock classic heaven knows.

a) My Uncle John taught his parrot to sing the words from the old rock classic Heaven Knows.
b) My uncle John taught his parrot to sing the words from the old rock classic Heaven Knows.
c) My Uncle John taught his parrot to sing the words from the old rock classic heaven knows.
d) My Uncle John taught his parrot to sing the words from the Old Rock Classic Heaven Knows.

10. raksmay wants to work for a large tech company such as intel or ibm.

a) Raksmay wants to work for a large Tech company such as Intel or IBM.
b) Raksmay wants to work for a large tech company such as intel or ibm.
c) Raksmay wants to work for a large tech company such as Intel or IBM.
d) Raksmay wants to work for a large Tech company such as intel or ibm.

Capitalise the following paragraph.

The Bold King

one thousand years ago, there was a king. king john lived in his castle in a long distant country called almadanis. almadanis was located in the southern valley near a large river which was called the romtong river. this river provided the people with fresh water, lots of fish, and large amounts of fruit and vegetables.

one day, as the people celebrated the annual harvest festival, a thunder storm came and flooded the river. the romtong overflowed and many houses were destroyed. as a result, many of the citizens of almadanis died from hunger and disease. when the water receded, the king called for his royal horses, so he could see the damage first hand. he began in the south and travelled through his entire country. he asked, "why are the people hungry?" the king's royal advisor answered, "they don't have any food." the king was upset and confused because he had always provided for his people. he responded, "then cultivate the fields and give them food."

king john asked, "why are the people so thirsty?" his royal advisor again responded, "because there is no clean water to drink." the king snapped back, "well dig wells and give them water!"

while he was returning, another thunder storm developed, and a hurricane destroyed his castle. when the king returned to his home, he asked the crying servants, "what happened?" the servants explained that nothing remained; everything was completely destroyed.

king John looked puzzled. he commanded, "well! then let's build a new castle."

in the years that followed, the king moved his entire country to the northern hills of aldamanis and rebuilt the country to its former glory.

3.   Identifying Subjects, Verbs, and Prepositional Phrases

Underline the subject, circle the verb, and put parentheses around all of the prepositional phrases.

1. Mrs Hung later became the director of the gallery.

2. It rained hard during the evening.

3. I would like to buy a green coat likes yours.

4. For my holiday, I went to Kompong Soam.

5. They lived down the road from us.

6. The field of rice swayed in the morning breeze.

7. Near the edge of the river, a single Kookaburra sang in a tree.

8. Many Australians fly to Bali for their summer vacation.

9. The bank robbers hid for a month in an abandoned house.

10. Each of us needs a little more time.

11. One of the cows is limping.

12. Open the cupboard and put these shoes inside the box.

13. On the last day of our holiday, we climbed Mt. Cook.

14. A flight from Cambodia to Thailand only takes an hour and a half.

15. My great grandmother slept quietly with her dog.

16. Korng and Suching were the best athletes on the team.

17. What is the name of your favourite movie?

18. A house of guests usually means a lot of work.

19. Start before midday.

20. Father took me to the pharmacy in the mall.

4.   Simple Sentences

Identify the type of single sentence.

1. My best friend is coming over to my house to visit me.

   a) SV
   b) SSV
   c) SVV
   d) SSVV

2. Two sweet little puppies looked up and woofed at me from inside the box.

   a) SV
   b) SSV
   c) SVV
   d) SSVV

3. At the stroke of midnight, he turned into a ghost.

   a) SV
   b) SSV
   c) SVV
   d) SSVV

4. The boy and dog ran and played in the park.

   a) SV
   b) SSV
   c) SVV
   d) SSVV

5. On Fridays and Saturdays, I usually go to work.

a) SV
b) SSV
c) SVV
d) SSVV

6. On Sundays, I play golf and eat with friends.

a) SV
b) SSV
c) SVV
d) SSVV

7. The cool, deep, blue ocean lapped onto the beach in front of me.

a) SV
b) SSV
c) SVV
d) SSVV

8. Will you have a coffee and lunch with me?

a) SV
b) SSV
c) SVV
d) SSVV

9. My best friend likes to paint and read.

a) SV
b) SSV
c) SVV
d) SSVV

10. My mother and father never eat and drink at the movies.

a) SV
b) SSV
c) SVV
d) SSVV

5.   Subject Verb Agreement

Cross out the prepositional phrase, underline the subject, and circle the correct verb that agrees with the subject.

1. The people in front of the counter (like, likes) to joke around with the staff.

2. Two men on my bowls team always (score, scores) over 30.

3. The noise from the airport sometimes (hurt, hurts) my ears.

4. A Big Mac hamburger (contain, contains) 32 grams of fat.

5. The instructions for downloading my book (is, are) easy to follow.

6. Where (is, are) the keys to the house.

7. Underneath that big rock (live, lives) thousands of red ants.

8. There (was, were) three people in front of me at the supermarket.

9. Why (does, do) cats always screech the loudest at 3 am?

10. Inside each box, There (is, are) twelve biscuits

11. The boys from Johnn Septimus Roe (is, are) arriving early today.

12. The heads of government (arrive, arrives) for the meeting.

13. The bag of tennis balls (is, are) on the table.

14. The boxes of highlighters (is, are) in the cupboard.

15. A shipment of washing machines (is, are) due next week.

16. The little monkey (slide, slides) down the tree.

17. The problems with Sambat (has, have) to be solved.

18. Sambat, together with Sokieng, (dance, dances) wonderfully.

19. The boys, as well as Mealea, (watch, watches) quietly.

20. High on the closet shelf (is, are) several colourfully wrapped birthday presents.

6.   Coordinating Conjunctions

Combine the sentences using a comma and coordinating conjunction.

1. I don't want to argue with you. I don't want to give in.

2. He had a lot of friends. He was a friendly person.

3. She had a cute puppy. She lost it.

4. He studied hard for the test. He got the top score.

5. Raksmey can cook omelette. Mealea can't cook eggs at all.

6. We can go to Kompong Soam. We can go to Kep.

7. Korng moved to Phnom Penh. Then he moved back home again.

8. He didn't want to be late. He left early.

9. Keang runs around the park every day. He swims on Sundays.

10. You can choose a strawberry milk shake. You can choose a chocolate milk shake.

11. I don't like green. I don't like pink.

12. I am the smarter than my sister. She received a higher score on the quiz.

13. Mealea spent all her money when she went the King Kong sale. She went back the next day.

14. Sivleng is going to the beach. She worries about being sunburnt.

15. We sang very well. We didn't win the singing contest.

16. Either we will win. They will win.

17. He was a popular prime minister. All of his countrymen loved him.

18. I wanted to camp on the beach. My mother wouldn't let me.

19. You can cruise to Hong Kong. You can cruise to Bali.

20. The baby is always crying. He is always hungry.

7.   Compound Sentences

Fill in the blank with the correct coordinating conjunction to form a compound sentence.

1. She wanted to come, _____ she didn't have time. (but, nor)

2. I opened the curtains, _____ I looked out. (and, yet)

3. He wasn't downstairs, _____ was he upstairs. (or, nor)

4. The sun had set, _____ It was still light outside. (or, yet)

5. I read the article, _____ I didn't quite understand it. (but, or)

6. He could not go to the concert, _____ he didn't have enough money. (for, so)

7. Sambat didn't have enough money to fly to Siem Reap, _____ he took the bus. (so, for)

8. Korng bought his father a new motorbike, _____ his father loved it. (but, and)

9. I don't work hard at school, ___ do I get good grades. (or, nor)

10. I don't get good grades at school, _____ I don't study hard (or, for)

11. I don't study hard, _____ I don't get good grades. (so, for)

12. It is starting to rain outside, _____ I think I'll bring my umbrella. (or, so)

13. For dinner, I ate a hamburger, _____ I ate a piece of cake. (and, or)

14. Students are often late for class, _____ they have to park some distance from school. (for, yet)

15. I bought three pens, _____ I lost two of them. (and, so)

16. Now I will have to buy two more, _____ I have enough money. (yet, but)

17. Mealea forgot her school lunch, _____ her mother took it to school. (for, so)

18. I have never visited Preah Vihear, _____ have I visited Mondolkirri. (nor, and)

19. Sokleng caught a snake, _____ his father said he couldn't keep it. (and, but)

20. Lyly could watch TV tonight, _____ she could read a book. (so, or)

8.   Commas

Re-write these sentences adding commas.

1. Tomorrow we will take a trip to the beach.

2. I like volleyball but my sister on the other hand doesn't.

3. The capital of Australia is Canberra ACT.

4. The guests sang *Happy Birthday* as the cake was being cut.

5. Mealea for example likes to study hard.

6. The SEA games will begin on Thursday May 15 2015.

7. My three favourite foods are fish and chips hamburgers and pizza.

8. After 5 minutes you can come in.

9. You however are very wrong.

10. Sivlieng cannot cook nor can she dance.

11. I need to contact Mealea Sivlong and Sambat.

12. I'm sorry but I didn't understand the question.

13. When my brother graduated from university he got a good job.

14. I washed the dishes while my mother cleaned the house.

15. I have to go to the market take some money from the bank and get my hair cut.

16. When I get to the shopping centre I will go to the food hall.

17. I enjoy studying science but I don't enjoy geography.

18. Today is Thursday 15 May 2015.

19. My friend lives in Phnom Penh Cambodia.

20. Next week while I work you can visit your mother in Siem Reap and your aunt in Battambong.

9.   Sentence Errors

Choose the correct answer.

1. Written 4 books in three years

   a) Fragment
   b) Comma Slice
   c) Run on
   d) OK

2. My motorbike is too old.

   a) Fragment
   b) Comma Slice
   c) Run on
   d) OK

3. Everyone I know always late.

   a) Fragment
   b) Comma Slice
   c) Run on
   d) OK

4. My mother cooks my breakfast she drives me to school.

   a) Fragment
   b) Comma Slice
   c) Run on
   d) OK

5. When school is finished, she picks me up, then she cooks dinner.

a) Fragment
b) Comma Slice
c) Run on
d) OK

6. Before we go to class.

a) Fragment
b) Comma Slice
c) Run on
d) OK

7. I have a dog.

a) Fragment
b) Comma Slice
c) Run on
d) OK

8. Doing a good job.

a) Fragment
b) Comma Slice
c) Run on
d) OK

9. During football games, my brother eats 4 hotdogs, then has a pizza.

a) Fragment
b) Comma Slice
c) Run on
d) OK

10. We played football after school Then I went home.

a) Fragment
b) Comma Slice
c) Run on
d) OK

Read the following text and correct any sentence errors you find.

11.

Ever since Sokunthea looked at Sarak's exam paper. She has felt guilt. Every time she sees Sarak, wonders why she passed and Sarak failed. Sarak is a good student, never fails exams. Whereas she is not a good student she usually fails. The world works in mysterious ways.

12.

The American Cactus

No symbol of the great American desert is more recognisable than the cactus. Thriving in dryness and heat that would kill most other plants, cactuses can live for long stretches of time without water, precious rainwater is stored in their stems. Although a bane to humans, the narrow needles on most kinds of cactuses shield the plant from attack by animals. Several types of cactus common throughout the Southwest of the US. Opuntias, usually called prickly pear, the oldest known cactus. They grow broad pads that are flavourful They are used in many South-western and Latin American recipes. The graceful organ pipe species, also prized for its tasty fruit. Chollas are common hikers and campers hate them because their long and painful thorns break off easily and are difficult to remove from flesh. The giant saguaro is often likened to a human standing with arms raised and bent at the elbows. The saguaro can grow as high as 17 m, it may live for more than 200 years. All of these common types of cactus are endangered as towns move closer to the desert, bringing pollution and clearing of entire groves. Disease, worms, and a growing rodent population, all additional threats to the silent strength and defiant beauty of desert cactus.

10. Apostrophes

Correct each sentence adding apostrophes in the right places.

1. Whos the Liberal representative for prime minister this year?

2. The bear had its foot locked tightly by the traps teeth.

3. My friends car is an old Toyota, and its just about ready to fall apart.

4. In two weeks time, well begin school again.

5. You didnt hear! Theyre leaving in the morning.

6. The workers cars are parked under the building.

7. The Smiths children looked so disappointed.

8. Its important that children learn their address.

9. He didnt hear his childrens cries for help.

10. Your address has three 3s, and your phone number has three 3s.

11. He didnt say when he would arrive at Sambats house.

12. Its such a glorious day.

13. The shop sells ladies handbags and shoes.

14. The two girls handbags were lying on the rivers bank.

15. Stephens mothers house is next to his sisters house.

16. The green grocers shop is at the supermarket.

17. For some reason, I always use two ps in the word apostrophes.

18. A dogs bark is far worse than its bite.

19. The company is going ahead with its plans to build the companys head office.

20. Young chidrens clothing is on the second floor of the department store.

11.   Punctuation (Putting it together)

Read each paragraph and correct all the punctuation mistakes.

1.

Once upon a time there was a huge hairy fat monster that lived in the hills of aldamanis. It was not well liked and feared people tried to kill it with arrows swords and spears but the monster always shouted drooled grunted and wailed it did not die. One day a fearsome warrior appeared wearing armour of steal and pierced the creature with his mystical sword. The huge beast screamed dropped to the ground coiled over and suddenly died the happy king rewarded the knight with gold silver diamonds and rubies and the kingdom lived happily ever after.

2.

While english is the first spoken language and sometimes the second spoken language in many countries it certainly isnt spoken by all of its residents. Moreover those people who speak english in foreign countries are not necessarily able to read it unless you have your companys documents translated and localized you will always look like a foreign company. You risk having your business ignored or misunderstood if your company image is important to you quality translation is crucial to be successful in a foreign country.

3.

When sambat takes an exam he follows this special procedure. First he tries to find a seat in the exam room away from the other examinees. He might sit at the back of the room or he might sit at the front of the room. Next he gets his supplies such as pencils pape, and pens ready. Sometimes if the exam allows he brings his calculator or textbook finally he sits quietly for a minute or two before the exam begins to relax and clear his thoughts before starting the exam

4.

One of my favourite pastimes is travelling abroad as a result i decided to get a job that paid me to travel. because I couldnt afford to pay for my expensive habit. I finally got a job working for a company called off shore tours where I lead bicycle trips for tourists it was really a hard job but I got to spend three months living and working in cambodias southern beaches. Furthermore I went to angkor wat. It was really great travelling around Cambodia however the job was too much work and not enough free time to do what I wanted to do Therefore while the job fed my travelling habit I knew it wasnt the right job for me.

5.

The robber climbed through the window crept up the stairs and looked into the bedroom. The owner of the house shouted as loudly as she could but no one heard her. The phone wasnt too far away yet there wasnt much could do to get to the phone. After she switched on all the lights man ran away in a panic. When the police arrived they took notes checked the house and ran tests. All they told her to do was to put locks on her windows.

12.   Topic and Supporting Sentences

Choose the most appropriate topic sentence for the following paragraph.

1.

_____

The head has a pair of antennae and a pair of compound eyes. The thorax is the middle region of the body, and it bears the legs and wings. The abdomen contains many body organs such as the heart, respiratory system, digestive system, and reproductive system. Even though there are many different sizes, shapes, and colours of insects, they all have the same body.

a)   The thorax is the middle region of the body.
b)   The abdomen contains many body organs.
c)   All insects have three main body parts: the head, the thorax, and the abdomen.
d)   The head has a pair of antennae and a pair of compound eyes.

2.

_____

I went to visit my aunt and my cousins in Sydney. My aunt is a dance teacher. I took dance lessons from her. I went to see the famous Tauranga Park Zoo with my cousins. We went to the beach almost every day. We stayed up late playing card games and watching TV. I wished my holiday would never end.

a)   I wished my holiday would never end.
b)   I had a wonder holiday this year.
c)   We went to the beach almost every day.
d)   My aunt is a dance teacher.

3.

_____

Sokeng was very upset today. She lost her favourite toy that she got on her birthday. It was not an ordinary present. It was a present from her best friend. Her fiends name is Lyly. She is the same age as Sokeng. They play together after school every day. Their favourite game is to dress up dolls. Sokeng's father told her he would buy her a new toy. That still did not make her happy.

a) Their favourite game is to dress up dolls.
b) They play together after school every day.
c) That still did not make her happy.
d) Sokeng was very upset today.

Read the paragraph and then answer the questions.

The City is Dangerous

When you move to the city or if you are a tourist in a city abroad, you should pay attention to your personal safety. Compared to living in the countryside, living in the city is dangerous, so to avoid becoming a victim and use your common sense.

Do not stand on street corners looking at guide books. Instead, go sit down in a coffee shop to study them. Keep a map and the address of your hotel with you at all times to prevent getting lost. If you look like you are lost, you make an easy target for a robber.

Avoid wandering alone at night especially in a bar or club area. Always go with friends and stay on well-lit streets, and do not go out alone to exercise early in the morning.

Do not wear fancy clothes, accessories, or jewellery. Stay alert to avoid pickpockets, muggers, or bag snatchers. These are kinds of sneak attack robbers. Do not think that because you are in a nice neighbourhood or a busy shopping centre that you are safe. People might follow you from your hotel, attack you in a city park, or even a store parking lot.

Of course, if you are confronted by an armed robber, you should never argue or resist. Do what you are told and report it to the police latter.

Whether you are in a city in your home country or travelling overseas, stay alert and stay safe.

4. What is the topic sentence?

    a) Compared to living in the countryside, living in the city is dangerous, so to avoid becoming a victim and use your common sense.
    b) When you move to the city or if you are a tourist in a city abroad, you should pay attention to your personal safety.
    c) Avoid wandering alone at night, especially in a bar or club area
    d) Whether you are in a city in your home country or travelling overseas, stay alert and stay safe.

5. Which is not a main idea of the story?

    a) Do not stand on street corners looking guide books.
    b) Avoid wandering alone at night or in the morning.
    c) Do not wear fancy clothes, accessories, or jewellery.
    d) People might follow you from your hotel or attack you in a city park or even a store parking lot.

6. Which would make the best substitute title for this story?

    a) Stay alert! Stay Safe.

    b) Robbers are dangerous.

    c) Don't travel alone.

    d) Should I go on holiday?

7. What is the concluding sentence?

_____

8. Does the concluding sentence summarize the main idea or restate the topic sentence?

_____

Read the topic sentences below. Write a topic question. Then use the topic question to determine 4 main ideas for the topic.

9. Smoking in restaurants should be prohibited.

Topic Question:

_____

    a) _____

    b) _____

    c) _____

    d) _____

10. International students sometimes have difficulty taking notes in class.

Topic Question:

_____

    a) _____

    b) _____

    c) _____

    d) _____

13. Paragraph Unity

Cross out the sentences that do not support the topic, thus destroying paragraph unity.

1. Topic Sentence: Restoring antique wooden furniture is challenging but rewarding.

- Antiques are very expensive, especially at auctions.
- Before stripping the wood, it is important to identify how old the wood is.
- Knowing how old the antique is can make a difference in the type of restorer you use to clean and polish the wood.
- The shine of the wood when you have finished is superb.
- Antiques dealers sometime overprice their goods.
- Chairs are the most difficult to restore because of the angles and curves.

2. Topic Sentence: Parent's attention focuses on the safety of children's toys.

- Most tricycles now have handlebars covered with plastic.
- Playing marbles is a favourite children's game.
- Too many toys for small children come with small pieces which can be put into their mouths and cause choking.
- Manufacturers now use non-toxic materials on toys.
- Toys with sharp edges that may cut or scratch should be recalled.
- Children enjoy playing with toys they see on TV.

3. Topic Sentence: Folktales are more than just simple fairy tales; they teach important values of the culture.

- Many libraries have a story telling period.

- The principles of good and evil are told in words children can understand.
- Nothing is more enjoyable than a good mystery.
- Many stories tell of the power of love over hate and good over evil.
- The characters are usually one dimensional.

4.

Although my sister is 3 years older than myself, we share a lot of similarities. We both have bright yellow hair. I don't like computer games at all, however, she does. We both play softball, and we are both catchers. Both of us enjoy reading. Since we have many similarities, we do many things together.

5.

My school day is filled with activity. First of all, the day begins with form room. Then I go to my English class which is really enjoyable. Before lunch, I always got to my sport class. After that, I have lunch in the school canteen where I meet my friends. In the afternoon, I have 3 other subjects to study. By the end of the day, after being so busy, I just want to sit and relax with my friends.

6.

Many Khmer families have different traditions for Khmer New Year. Some families may go on vacation. Other families may prepare a feast at home and invite relatives to join them. Some families open Christmas presents. Each family celebrates Khmer New Year differently.

7.

Adventure travel is the latest fad in the tourism industry. Normal people do not want to spend their 4 week holiday on a tropical beach anymore. More and more people are choosing to spend their holiday rafting down a river, hiking through rain forest, or climbing the world's mountains. People of all ages are now choosing educational tour for their vacation.

8.

All students can improve their grades if they do their homework. By doing your homework that your teacher assigns you, you can learn the things your teacher is trying to teach you. You will be prepared for the next lesson. Study hard at home. By keeping up with your homework, you will find each new lesson easier to follow, and your grades will soon start improving.

9.

Teachers should take some common sense precautions to avoid cheating. They should separate students by at least one seat. They should watch the class closely during the exam. The best place to stand is at the back of the room, so students cannot see where teacher is looking. Teachers must make the rules clear for anyone caught cheating. Using this approach will reduce incidences of cheating.

10.

Indoor plants are both decorative and functional. With minimal preparation and design, people can transform their home into light and airy places. Many indoor plants bloom all year round. As well as adding beauty to the area, green plants release oxygen into the atmosphere. Flower arranging is a Japanese art.

14.   Paragraph Coherence

a)   Consistent Nouns and Pronouns

Change the following passage to plural subject noun and find and fix the pronouns that are not consistent with the nouns they refer to.

1.

When a tax payer is waiting to receive a tax refund from the Taxation Department, you begin to notice what time the mailman comes. If a taxpayer doesn't receive his or her tax refund within four weeks of filing the return, they may not have filled in the form correctly. For example, taxpayers who don't include their tax file number on the return will have to wait longer for his or her tax refund. If they have made errors on the form, you will have to wait, and Taxation Department may even audit you. This may cause delays of weeks or months. Even if you file your tax return on time, the Taxation Department may still delay your refund because the department is extremely busy at the end of the financial year.

Find and fix the pronouns that are not consistent with the nouns they refer to.

2.
Since I moved into my new flat last year, I have stopped making my bed. Except on Saturdays when I wash and change the sheets. Even though, some people think this is a bad habit, I have some good reason for not making my bed in the morning. Firstly, he or she is not concerned with keeping a neat and tidy bedroom because they don't have any visitors. If there is a visitor, then I can dash into the bedroom and quickly make the bed. Furthermore, they find nothing uncomfortable about an unmade bed. In contrast, I enjoy creating a comfy, cosy spot before

drifting off to a slumber. They think that well-made beds are uncomfortable. Most importantly, I think making a bed in the morning is a waste of our time. I'd prefer to be checking my email or working on my book.

b)   *Transition Signals*

i.   Using Time Order

Underline the time order words and phrases in the following paragraph.

How boil an Egg

Boling an egg the right way is not difficult if you follow my directions. First of all, take the egg out of the refrigerator 15 minutes before you want to boil it. Next, grab some bread and toast it. Make sure the bread is well toasted, and there is a lot of butter spread from corner to corner. Once buttered, cut the toast into fingers about 1 cm wide. Now place a pot of water on the stove, light the gas, and set it to maximum. Bring the pot of water to the boil, and then turn the gas down to medium. After 15 minutes, grab a spoon and insert the egg into the boiling water, and then set the egg timer for 4 minutes. While you wait for the egg to cook, get yourself an egg cup. When the egg timer sounds, turn of the gas, remove the egg, and let it cool for two minutes. Finally, place the egg into the egg cup and cut the top off. You'll be amazed how good the soft boiled egg is with toasted soldiers and a little salt.

ii.   Using Space order

Underline the space order words and phrases in the following paragraph.

The Stirling Ranges

Standing at one of the lookouts in the Stirling Ranges, Western Australia, a few hardy hikers take in the view during a bitter and cold July afternoon. Off to the left of the lookout, there was a grove of petrified trees which were once green and everlasting. The last rays of sunshine sparkled through bare branches of the grove of trees. In front of them, dark rain clouds began to form. The deepening clouds began to move towards the coast and the rain storm would wash out to sea. To the right of the lookout, the trail which they had used seemed like an endless climb, and they wondered how they made it to the lookout. As they took in the view, they all agreed the hike was well worth it.

iii.   Process transitions

What are the steps to grow a strawberry plant? Put the sequence into the correct order and write the paragraph using process order (time order).

1. _____ Put the plant into a pot.
2. _____ Take the strawberry plant out of its container.
3. _____ Put the potting mixture into a pot.
4. _____ Water the soil.
5. _____ Make a hole in the soil.
6. _____ Remove the dark and dead leaves.
7. _____ Fertilize your strawberry plant once a week.
8. _____ Press the soil down firmly.

c)   *Logical division of ideas*

Read the paragraph and answer the question on logical order in paragraphs or essays

Animals in Zoos

There are 3 advantages and 3 disadvantages for animals living in zoos. The first advantage of living in a zoo is the animals are kept separated from their natural enemies. The cages protect the animals, thus, they can live without fear of being killed or maimed. The second advantage is the animals are fed regularly, so they do not have to forage or hunt for food, and they don't go hungry when food is hard to find. The final advantage is the animals' health is well taken care of. All the animals receive medical checks on a regular basis by a veterinarian. As all the animals' needs are catered for in zoos, they live a healthy and happy life. However, despite the 3 advantages, there are 3 disadvantages. The first and most important disadvantage is because they don't have to forage or hunt for their food, they can become board, unhappy, and even aggressive. A second disadvantage is patrons' visits to the zoo can cause some animals to catch human illnesses unless they are protected by walls of glass. In addition, zoo visitors regularly throw human food or scraps to the animals. This inadvertently can kill the animals, or they can become seriously sick. In short, although animals living in zoos can lead a healthy and protected life, the animals can also become bored or perhaps die from human illnesses.

1. What is the topic sentence? Underline the topic sentence.

2. How many advantages does the author list? What are they (underline them)?

3. What transition words and phrases introduce the advantages (double underline them)?

4. Underline the sentence that introduces the disadvantages. What transition phrase or signal is used?

5. How many disadvantages does the author list? What are they (underline them)?

6. What transition words and phrases are used to introduce the disadvantages (double underline them)?

7. What transitional signal is use to introduce the concluding sentence (underline it)?

15.   Clauses

Add an independent clause to the dependent clauses.

1. When I graduate from high school

_____.

2. *The Academic Writing Skills* series, which are good books,

_____.

3. _____ until Stephen
moved to Cambodia.

4. After the game was over

_____.

5. Since I met you in English class

_____.

6. _____ because I didn't
think before I spoke.

7. _____until I
call you on Saturday.

8. _____ whom I assist as a student aide
during my free time

9. Although we were lost

_____.

10. Before you apply to university

_____.

16. Appositives

Underline the appositive in each sentence.

1. My oldest son, the policeman, will be visiting me next week.

2. Sambat, the author, is very attached to his sister.

3. Apple, a world-wide company, is considering a new iPhone release.

4. An above average student and talented football player Sambat made his father proud.

5. The extremely popular Khmer film Tum Teau was widely criticized for its script.

6. My next door neighbour Mr. Dew is a really good musician.

7. James Dew, Mr. Dew's son, owns a recording studio.

8. Atari, a toy and game manufacturer, came out with Pong, the first video game, in 1972.

9. On Mars, the closest planet to earth, scientists hope to find water.

10. The motorbike a Honda Wave was badly damaged.

Underline the appositives in the paragraph.

Funny Names

The local florist and his wife had a sense of humour when naming their children, three daughters and a son. Their eldest daughter, Lyly, didn't mind being named after a flower. Soken, her best friend, agreed that Lyly was a normal name. By the time their second daughter was born, the florist and his wife, a creative couple, used an unusual name. They named their daughter after the Chrysanthemum, the florist favourite flower. Although it was a difficult name, she didn't really mind it either. Most of her friends just call her Chrissie. By the time daughter number three arrived, her parents decided to be really unique. They named her Delphinium. This youngest daughter, a future biologist, was called Della by her friends. When they had their last child, a boy, they wondered what to call him. They couldn't think of a good blooming plant name for their son. Looking around the floral shop, the florist found something they could use. The unlikely plant a cactus made the florist think of a name more suited to a boy. They bought their new born son, Saguaro, home and showed him to his three sisters. Saguaro, the youngest of the florist's children, turned out to be a handsome young man with no thorns at all.

17.   Complex Sentences

a) Adverb Clauses (Subordinating Clauses)

Join the two sentences using a logical subordinator that shows the sentence relationship.

1. Sambat suggested going to Kirrirom. It was hot and humid in Phnom Penh.

2. They arrived at Kirrirom. They bought a map of the area's trails.

3. Sengly chose a short trail. Sambat chose a longer more difficult trail.

4. Sengly agreed to go on the more difficult trail. Sambat promised to pay for the hotel room.

5. They started out on the trail. They left the trail and walked some distance into the forest.

6. Sengly felt a pain in his arm. He suggested stopping and resting for a while.

7. Sengly took off his shirt. He found a tick had attached itself to his arm.

8. Both Sambat and Sengly knew ticks carry diseases. They read newspapers and watch TV nature shows.

9. Ticks, including a few in Kirrirom, carry Lyme disease. Sengly wasn't worried.

10. He removed the tick immediately. He will be less likely to contact the disease.

11. I really enjoyed the concert. The music was too loud.

12. Mealea needs to learn English. I will teach her.

13. Stephen played tennis very well. He was very young.

14. Mouy Leng wants to get a new job. She is preparing for the interview now.

15. Vannda thinks he will buy the car. He just wants to check with his wife first.

16. William has been working 40 hours a week. There is a big class presentation next week.

17. I usually exercise in the morning. I leave for work at 7.30 am.

18. Sen Kosal didn't have much money. He bought the motorbike.

19. Sen Kosal enjoys going to the movies. He enjoys going with his friend Lisa. Lisa visits once a week.

20. During rainy season, we have a lot of rain. I put the patio furniture in the garage.

b)   Adjective Clauses (Relative Clauses)

Fill in the blanks with an appropriate adjective clause.

1. Sambat, _____ plays football every day, won the competition.

2. The video game _____ you lent me had a virus _____ affected my computer.

3. Where is my English book _____ was on the desk?

4. Instead of watching TV, I prefer playing computer games, _____ are more interesting.

5. What was the name of the girl _____ you saw on Facebook.

6. The new tennis coach _____ none of the players like wants the team to practise more.

7. The school has decided to call a parent meeting _____ will start at 6 pm tonight.

8. Sambat, _____ house is near the park, goes jogging every day.

9. In May, I'm going to Perth, _____ is where my sister lives.

10. My English teacher, _____ had an accident, is back in class today.

Combine the two sentences into one complex sentence using relative pronouns.

11. I tried to talk to the girl. Her motorbike had run out petrol in front of my house.

12. Where is the attendant? We need his services.

13. Sokleng is a tuk tuk driver. He lives on the corner.

14. Where is the man? He ordered the coffee.

15. The banana is inedible. It fell behind the couch four days ago.

16. The tourist comes from Cambodia. We met him in Siem Reap last week.

17. Where is the bottle of orange juice. I bought the bottle last night.

18. I borrowed these English books for my assignment. They have more than 300 pages long.

19. Sokeng is a wealthy man. He rarely worries about the cost of things.

20. I saw a painting on the wall. It was painted at Angkor Wat.

21. She married a man. She met the man on the bus.

22. He has written a book. I have forgotten the books name.

23. In 2005, he met Lyly. He later married her.

24. Dr. Smith is a person. I don't have much time for him.

25. We listened to a speech yesterday. The speech was interesting.

26. The student is in my English class. You just met them.

27. The chair was wet. I sat on it.

28, Khmer New year is a time. Khmer people celebrate the new theveda.

29. Stephen tutors ESL students. They need help with English writing.

30. Diamonds are valuable gems. Diamonds are mined in Cambodia.

18. Simple, Compound, or Complex

Choose the correct answer.

1. After dinner, we go bed when we have finished our homework.

- a) Simple
- b) Compound
- c) Complex

2. Mealea likes Stephen's friend, and she also likes his nephew.

- a) Simple
- b) Compound
- c) Complex

3. Before going to work, I take my big black dog to run in the park.

- a) Simple
- b) Compound
- c) Complex

4. Sambat and Lyly ride their bikes before lunch.

- a) Simple
- b) Compound
- c) Complex

5. The teacher and the student met in the lab which is near the library.

- a) Simple
- b) Compound

c) Complex

6. After I wake up, I eat breakfast and brush my teeth.

a) Simple
b) Compound
c) Complex

7. Before midnight, before the ghost came out, they set up cameras and recorders.

a) Simple
b) Compound
c) Complex

8. Many Australian soldiers fought in the war, and they received medals for valour.

a) Simple
b) Compound
c) Complex

9. She dropped the saucepan and the plate.

a) Simple
b) Compound
c) Complex

10. The vice admiral gave a speech after the prime minister arrived.

a) Simple
b) Compound
c) Complex

19. Sentence Combining

Combine each of the sentence groups into one sentence. You can create a simple, compound, or complex sentence but do not change the meaning of the sentence. Your sentences will for a connected paragraph. Write the paragraph containing the 9 sentences.

___Our Fridge___

1.
I share a fridge with my flat mate.

2.
My side of the fridge is disorganised.
My side of the fridge is grimy.
My side of the fridge is discoloured.

3.
A box of eggs sits on the fridge shelf.
The fridge shelf is the top one.
The eggs are broken.

4.
Sticks of celery and cold meats are on the fridge shelf.
The fridge shelf is the second one.
They share it with the tomatoes and bread.

5.
The celery is wilted.
The cold meats smell.
The bread is stale.
The tomatoes are yucky.

6.

Slices of pepperoni pizza sit on the fridge shelf.
The pepperoni pizza is leftover.
Lasagne sits on the fridge shelf
The lasagne sits on top of the pepperoni pizza.
They sit on the third fridge shelf.

7,
The bottom fridge crisper contains a variety of food.
The variety is intriguing.
The variety is of plastic bags and cardboard boxes.
The food is from Lucky Burger.
The food is from KFC.
The food is from Taco Bill.

8.
A small pond covers the bottom of the fridge.
The small pond looks icky.
The small pond is brown.

9.
My flat mate and I are not the same.
We get along OK.

Combine each of the sentence groups into one sentence. You can create a simple, compound, or complex sentence but do not change the meaning of the sentence. Your sentences will for a connected paragraph. Write the paragraph containing the 8 sentences.

Sopheap's Story

1.
My name is Chetra.
My age is 13-years-old.

2.

I live in Phnom Penh.
My parents live in Phnom Penh.
My sister lives in Phnom Penh.
My sister's name is Sopheap.

3.
My sister goes to a school.
I go to a school.
The school is the same school.

4.
Sopheap is a normal girl.
Sopheap likes to tell stories
Sopheap tells the stories to people.
The stories are untrue.
The stories are about our family.

5.
She said our family comes from Australia.
She said we lived on the beach.
She said we rode kangaroos.
This happened last month.
For example, (put this expression first)

6.
The story is untrue.
The story is a complete fabrication.

7.
Our family was born in Cambodia.
(This applies to all our family).
We have never been to Australia.
Of course, (put this idea first)

8.
I wish Sopheap would stop telling stories.

The stories are embarrassing.

20.   Using Quotations

Use quotes where necessary to show what some said or wrote.

1. Are we there yet she asked.

2. The construction engineer told us the building would not collapse.

3. I'm tired the boy said and then drifted off to sleep.

4. We really should be going now she said.

5. Excuse me he said do you have a light.

6. Daddy can I have a banana he said.

7. The Prime minister yelled we must have peace.

8. Sambat said 'you can go now' his friend repeated.

9. The mother told her friend the child simply has a lot of energy.

10. I received a fail on my homework because I forgot to write my name on it.

21.   Answer Key

a) Capitals

1	2	3	4	5	6	7	8	9	10
D	B	D	A	C	A	B	D	A	C

The Bold King

One thousand years ago, there was a king. King John lived in his castle in a long distant country called Almadanis. Almadanis was located in the Southern valley near a large river which was called the Romtong river. This river provided the people with fresh water, lots of fish, and large amounts of fruit and vegetables.

One day, as the people celebrated the annual harvest festival, a thunder storm came and flooded the river. The Romtong overflowed and many houses were destroyed. As a result, many of the citizens of Almadanis died from hunger and disease. When the water receded, the king called for his royal horses, so he could see the damage first hand. He began in the South and travelled through his entire country. He asked, "Why are the people hungry?" The king's royal advisor answered, "They don't have any food." The king was upset and confused because he had always provided for his people. He responded, "Then cultivate the fields and give them food."

King John asked, "Why are the people so thirsty?" His royal advisor again responded, "Because there is no clean water to drink." The king snapped back, "Well dig wells and give them water!"

While he was returning, another thunder storm developed, and a hurricane destroyed his castle. When the king returned to his home, he asked the crying servants, "What happened?" The servants explained that nothing remained; everything was completely destroyed.

King John looked puzzled. He commanded, "Well! Then let's build a new castle."

In the years that followed, the king moved his entire country to the Northern hills of Aldamanis and rebuilt the country to its former glory.

b) Subjects, verbs, and Prepositional Phrases

1. Mrs. Hung later became the director (of the gallery).

2. It rained hard (during the evening).

3. I would like to buy a green coat likes yours.

4. (For my holiday), I went (to Kompong Soam).

5. They lived (down the road) (from us).

6. The field (of rice) swayed (in the morning breeze).

7. (Near the edge) (of the river), a single Kookaburra sang (in a tree).

8. Many Australians fly (to Bali) (for their summer vacation).

9. The bank robbers hid (for a month) (in an abandoned house).

10. Each (of us) needs a little more time.

11. One (of the cows) is limping.

12. *You* Open the cupboard and put these shoes (inside the box).

13. (On the last day) (of our holiday), <u>we</u> climbed Mt. Cook.

14. <u>A flight</u> (from Cambodia) (to Thailand) only takes (an hour and a half).

15. <u>My great grandmother</u> slept quietly (with her dog).

16. <u>Korng and Suching</u> were the best athletes (on the team).

17. What is the name (of your favourite movie)?

18. <u>A house</u> (of guests) usually means (a lot of work).

19. *You* Start (before midday).

20. <u>Father</u> took me (to the pharmacy) (in the mall).

c) *Simple Sentences*

1	2	3	4	5	6	7	8	9	10
A	C	A	D	A	C	A	B	C	D

d) *Subject Verb agreement*

1. <u>The people</u> ~~in front of the counter~~ (like, likes) to joke around ~~with the staff~~.

2. <u>Two men</u> ~~on my bowls team~~ always (score, scores) over 30.

3. <u>The noise</u> ~~from the airport~~ sometimes (hurt, hurts) my ears.

4. <u>A Big Mac hamburger</u> (contain, contains) 32 grams ~~of fat~~.

5. The instructions ~~for downloading my book~~ (is, (are)) easy to follow.

6. Where (is, (are)) the keys ~~to the house~~.

7. ~~Underneath that big rock~~ ((live), lives) thousands ~~of red ants~~.

8. There (was, (were)) three people ~~in front of me at the supermarket~~.

9. Why (does, (do)) cats always screech the loudest ~~at 3 am~~?

10. ~~Inside each box~~, There (is, (are)) twelve biscuits.

11. The boys ~~from Johnn Septimus Roe~~ (is, (are)) arriving early today.

12. The heads ~~of government~~ ((arrive), arrives) ~~for the meeting~~.

13. The bag ~~of tennis balls~~ ((is), are) ~~on the table~~.

14. The boxes ~~of highlighters~~ (is, (are)) ~~in the cupboard~~.

15 A shipment ~~of washing machines~~ ((is), are) due next week.

16. The little monkey (slide, (slides)) ~~down the tree~~.

17. The problems ~~with Samabat~~ (has, (have)) to be solved.

18. Sambat, ~~together with Sokieng~~, (dance, (dances)) wonderfully.

19. The boys, ~~as well as Mealea~~, ((watch), watches) quietly.

20. ~~High on the closet shelf~~ (is, (are)) several colourfully wrapped birthday presents.

e)   *Coordinating Conjunctions*

1. I don't want to argue with you, nor do I want to give in.

2. He had a lot of friends, for he was a friendly person.

3. She had a cute puppy, and she lost it.

4. He studied hard for the test, and he got the top score.

5. Raksmey can cook omelette, but Mealea can't cook eggs at all.

6. We can go to Kompong Soam, or we can go to Kep.

7. Korng moved to Phnom Penh, but then he moved back home again.

8. He didn't want to be late, so he left early.

9. Keang runs around the park every day, and he swims on Sundays.

10. You can choose a strawberry milk shake, or you can choose a chocolate milk shake.

11. I don't like green, nor do I like pink.

12. I am smarter than my sister, yet she received a higher score on the quiz.

13. Mealea spent all her money when she went the King Kong sale, yet she went back the next day.

14. Sivleng is going to the beach, but she worries about being sunburnt.

15. We sang very well, yet we didn't win the singing contest.

16. Either we will win, or they will win.

17. He was a popular prime minister, and all of his countrymen loved him.

18. I wanted to camp on the beach, but my mother wouldn't let me.

19. You can cruise to Hong Kong, or you can cruise to Bali.

20. The baby is always crying, for he is always hungry.

f)   Compound Sentences

1	but	11	so
2	and	12	so
3	nor	13	and
4	yet	14	for
5	but	15	and
6	for	16	but
7	so	17	so
8	and	18	nor
9	nor	19	but
10	for	20	or

g)   Commas

1. Tomorrow, we will take a trip to the beach.

2. I like volleyball, but my sister, on the other hand, doesn't.

3. The capital of Australia is Canberra, ACT.

4. The guests sang *Happy Birthday,* as the cake was being cut.

5. Mealea, for example, likes to study hard.

6. The SEA games will begin on Thursday, May 15, 2015.

7. My three favourite foods are fish and chips, hamburgers, and pizza.

8. After 5 minutes, you can come in.

9. You, however, are very wrong.

10 Sivlieng cannot cook, nor can she dance.

11. I need to contact Mealea, Sivlong, and Sambat.

12. I'm sorry, but I didn't understand the question.

13. When my brother graduated from university, he got a good job.

14. I washed the dishes, while my mother cleaned the house.

15. I have to go to the market, take some money from the bank, and get my hair cut.

16. When I get to the shopping centre, I will go to the food hall.

17. I enjoy studying science, but I don't enjoy geography.

18. Today is Thursday, 15 May, 2015.

19. My friend lives in Phnom Penh, Cambodia.

20. Next week, while I work, you can visit your mother in Siem Reap and your aunt in Battambong.

h)   *Sentence Errors*

1	Fragment	6	Fragment
2	OK	7	OK
3	Fragment	8	Fragment
4	Run on	9	Comma splice
5	Comma splice	10	Run on

11.

Ever since Sokunthea looked at Sarak's exam paper, she has felt guilt. Every time she sees Sarak, she wonders why she passed and Sarak failed. Sarak is a good student, and he never fails exams, whereas she is not a good student. She usually fails. The world works in mysterious ways.

12.

The Desert Cactus

No symbol of the great American desert is more recognisable than the cactus. Thriving in dryness and heat that would kill most other plants, cactuses can live for long stretches of time without water. Precious rainwater is stored in their stems. Although a bane to humans, the narrow needles on most kinds of cactuses shield the plant from attack by animals. There are several types of cactus common throughout the Southwest of the US. Opuntias, usually called prickly pear, is the oldest known cactus. They grow broad pads that are flavourful. They are used in many South-western and Latin American recipes. The graceful organ pipe species is also prized for its tasty fruit. Chollas are common, and hikers and campers hate them because their long and painful thorns break off easily and are difficult to remove from flesh. The giant saguaro is often likened to a human standing with arms raised and bent at the elbows. The saguaro can grow as high as 17 m, and it may live for more than 200 years. All of these common types of cactus are endangered as towns move closer to the desert bringing pollution and clearing of entire groves. Disease, worms, and a growing rodent population are all additional threats to the silent strength and defiant beauty of desert cactus.

i)   *Apostrophes*

1. Who's the Liberal representative for prime minister this year?

2. The bear had its foot locked tightly by the trap's teeth.

3. My friend's car is an old Toyota, and it's just about ready to fall apart.

4. In two weeks' time, we'll begin school again.

5. You didn't hear! They're leaving in the morning.

6. The workers' cars are parked under the building.

7. The Smiths' children looked so disappointed.

8. It's important that children learn their address.

9. He didn't hear his children's cries for help.

10. Your address has three 3's, and your phone number has three 3's.

11. He didn't say when he would arrive at Sambat's house.

12. It's such a glorious day.

13. The shop sells ladies' handbags and shoes.

14. The two girls' handbags were lying on the river's bank.

15. Stephen's mother's house is next to his sister's house.

16. The green grocer's shop is at the supermarket.

17. For some reason, I always use two p's in the word apostrophes.

18. A dog's bark is far worse than its bite.

19. The company is going ahead with its plans to build the company's head office.

20. Young children's clothing is on the second floor of the department store.

j)   *Punctuation Practice*

1.

Once upon a time, there was a huge, hairy, fat monster that lived in the hills of Aldamanis. It was not well liked and feared. People tried to kill it with arrows, swords, and spears, but the monster always shouted, drooled, grunted, and wailed. It did not die. One day, a fearsome warrior appeared wearing armour of steal and pierced the creature with his mystical sword. The huge beast screamed, dropped to the ground, coiled over, and suddenly died. The happy king rewarded the knight with gold, silver, diamonds, and rubies, and the kingdom lived happily ever after.

2.

While English is the first spoken language and sometimes the second spoken language in many countries, it certainly isn't spoken by all of its residents. Moreover, those people who speak English in foreign countries are not necessarily able to read it. Unless you have your company's documents translated and localized, you will always look like a foreign company. You risk having your business ignored or misunderstood. If your company image is important to you, quality translation is crucial to be successful in a foreign country.

3.

When Sambat takes an exam, he follows this special procedure. First, he tries to find a seat in the exam room away from the other examinees. He might sit at the back of the room, or he might sit at the front of the room. Next, he gets his supplies such as pencils, paper, and pens ready. Sometimes, if the exam allows, he brings his calculator or textbook. Finally, he sits quietly for a minute or two before the exam begins to relax and clear his thoughts before starting.

4.

One of my favourite pastimes is travelling abroad. As a result, I decided to get a job that paid me to travel because I couldn't afford to pay for my expensive habit. I finally got a job working for a company called Off Shore Tours where I lead bicycle trips for tourists. It was really a hard job, but I got to spend three months living and working in Cambodia's Southern beaches. Furthermore, I went to Angkor Wat. It was really great travelling around Cambodia, however, the job was too much work and not enough free time to do what I wanted to do. Therefore, while the job fed my travelling habit, I knew it wasn't the right job for me.

5.

The robber climbed through the window, crept up the stairs, and looked into the bedroom. The owner of the house shouted as loudly as she could, but no one heard her. The phone wasn't too far away, yet there wasn't much she could do to get to the phone. After she switched on all the lights, the man ran away in a panic. When the police arrived, they took notes, checked the house, and ran tests. All they told her to do was to put locks on her windows.

k) *Topic and Supporting Sentences*

1. All insects have three main body parts: the head, the thorax, and the abdomen.

2. I had a wonder holiday this year

3. Sokeng was very upset today

4. Compared to living in the countryside, living in the city is dangerous, so to avoid becoming a victim and use your common sense.

5. People might follow you from your hotel or attack you in a city park or even a store parking lot.

6. Stay alert! Stay Safe.

7. Whether you are in a city in your home country or travelling overseas, stay alert and stay safe.

8. Restate

Note: some answers may vary.

9. Topic question: Why should smoking in restaurants be prohibited?
    a) It pollutes the air.
    b) It can affect the dinner's appetites.
    c) It leaves a pungent odour.
    d) It can affect the health of others.

10. Topic question: Why do international students have difficulty taking notes in class?
    a) The teacher talks too fast.
    b) The students have poor listening skills.
    c) The students' vocabulary is limited.
    d) The students are slow at writing.

I)   *Paragraph Unity*

1. Topic Sentence: Restoring antique wooden furniture is challenging but rewarding.

- ~~Antiques are very expensive, especially at auctions.~~
- Before stripping the wood, it is important to identify how old the wood is.
- Knowing how old the antique is can make a difference in the type of restorer you use to clean and polish the wood.
- The shine of the wood when you have finished is superb.
- ~~Antiques dealers sometime overprice their goods.~~
- Chairs are the most difficult to restore because of the angles and curves.

2. Topic Sentence: Parent's attention focuses on the safety of children's toys.

- Most tricycles now have handlebars covered with plastic.

- ~~Playing marbles is a favourite children's game.~~
- Too many toys for small children come with small pieces which can be put into their mouths and cause choking.
- Manufacturers now use non-toxic materials on toys.
- Toys with sharp edges that may cut or scratch should be recalled.
- ~~Children enjoy playing with toys they see on TV.~~

3. Topic Sentence: Folktales are more than just simple fairy tales; they teach important values of the culture.

- ~~Many libraries have a story telling period.~~
- The principles of good and evil are told in words children can understand.
- Nothing is more enjoyable than a good mystery.
- Many stories tell of the power of love over hate and good over evil.
- ~~The characters are usually one dimensional.~~

4.

Although my sister is 3 years older than myself, we share a lot of similarities. We both have bright yellow hair. ~~I don't like computer games at all, however, she does.~~ We both play softball, and we are both catchers. Both of us enjoy reading. Since we have many similarities, we do many things together.

5.

My school day is filled with activity. First of all, the day begins with form room. Then I go to my English class ~~which is really enjoyable~~. Before lunch, I always got to my sport class. After that, I have lunch in the school canteen ~~where I meet my friends~~. In the afternoon, I have 3 other subjects to study. By the end of the day, after being so busy, I just want to sit and relax with my friends.

6.

Many Khmer families have different traditions for Khmer New Year. Some families may go on vacation. Other families may prepare a feast at home and invite relatives to join them. ~~Some families open Christmas presents~~. Each family celebrates Khmer New Year differently.

7.

Adventure travel is the latest fad in the tourism industry. Normal people do not want to spend their 4 week holiday on a tropical beach anymore. More and more people are choosing to spend their holiday rafting down a river, hiking through rain forest, or climbing the world's mountains. ~~People of all ages are now choosing educational tour for their vacation.~~

8.

All students can improve their grades if they do their homework. By doing your homework that your teacher assigns you, you can learn the things your teacher is trying to teach you. You will be prepared for the next lesson. ~~Study hard at home~~. By keeping up with your homework, you will find each new lesson easier to follow, and your grades will soon start improving.

9.

Teachers should take some common sense precautions to avoid cheating. They should separate students by at least one seat. They should watch the class closely during the exam. ~~The best place to stand is at the back of the room, so students cannot see where teacher is looking~~. Teachers must make the rules clear for anyone caught cheating. Using this approach will reduce incidences of cheating.

10.

Indoor plants are both decorative and functional. With minimal preparation and design, people can transform their home into light and airy places. Many indoor plants bloom all year round. As well as adding beauty to the area, green plants release oxygen into the atmosphere. ~~Flower arranging is a Japanese art.~~

m) *Paragraph Coherence*

i **Consistent Nouns and Pronouns**

1.

When tax payers are waiting to receive a tax refund from the Taxation Department, they begin to notice what time the mailman comes. If taxpayers don't receive their tax refund within four weeks of filing the return, they may not have filled in the form correctly. For example, taxpayers who don't include their tax file number on their return will have to wait longer for their tax refund. If they have made errors on the form, they will have to wait, and they may even be audited. This may cause delays of weeks or months. Even if they file their tax return on time, the Taxation Department may still delay their refund because the department is extremely busy at the end of the financial year.

2.

Since I moved into my new flat last year, I have stopped making my bed. Except on Saturdays, when I wash and change the sheets. Even though, some people think this is a bad habit, I have some good reason for not making my bed in the morning. Firstly, I am not concerned with keeping a neat and tidy bedroom because I don't have any visitors. If there is a visitor, then I can dash into the bedroom and quickly make the bed. Furthermore, I find nothing uncomfortable about an unmade bed. In contrast, I enjoy creating a comfy, cosy spot before drifting off to a slumber. I think that a well-made bed is uncomfortable. Most importantly,

I think making a bed in the morning is a waste of my time. I'd prefer to be checking my email or working on my book.

ii   Transition Signals

a. Using Time Order

How to Boil an Egg

Boling an egg the right way is not difficult if you follow my directions. <u>First of all</u>, take the egg out of the refrigerator 15 minutes before you want to boil it. <u>Next</u>, grab some bread and toast it. Make sure the bread is well toasted, and there is a lot of butter spread from corner to corner. <u>Once buttered</u>, cut the toast into fingers about 1 cm wide. <u>Now</u> place a pot of water on the stove, light the gas, and set it to maximum. Bring the pot of water to the boil, and then turn the gas down to medium. <u>After 15 minutes</u>, grab a spoon and insert the egg into the boiling water, and <u>then</u> set the egg timer for 4 minutes. <u>While you wait for the egg to cook</u>, get yourself an egg cup. <u>When the egg timer sounds</u>, turn of the gas, remove the egg, and let it cool for 2 minutes. <u>Finally</u>, place the egg into the egg cup and cut the top off. You'll be amazed how good the soft boiled egg is with toasted soldiers and a little salt.

b. Using Space order

The Stirling Ranges

Standing at one of the lookouts in the Stirling Ranges, Western Australia, a few hardy hikers take in the view during a bitter and cold July afternoon. <u>Off to the left of the lookout</u>, there was a grove of petrified trees which were once green and everlasting. The last rays of sunshine sparkled through bare branches of the grove of trees. <u>In front of them</u>, dark rain clouds began to form. The deepening clouds began to move towards the coast and the rain storm would wash out to sea. <u>To the right of the lookout</u>, the trail which they had used seemed like an endless climb, and they wondered how they made it to the lookout. As they took in the view, they all agreed the hike was well worth it.

c. Process transitions

Growing a Strawberry Plant

1. _____ Put the potting mixture into a pot.
2. _____ Make a hole in the potting mix soil.
3. _____ Take the strawberry plant out of its container.
4. _____ Remove the dark and dead leaves.
5. _____ Put the strawberry plant into the pot.
6. _____ Press the soil down firmly.
7. _____ Water the strawberry plant and soil.
8. _____ Fertilize your strawberry plant once a week.

    <u>First</u>, put some potting mixture into a pot. <u>Then</u> make a hole in the soil. <u>After that</u>, take the strawberry plant out of its container. Remove the dark and dead leaves. <u>Now</u> put the strawberry plant into the pot. Press the soil down firmly. <u>Finally</u>, water the strawberry plant and soil. Don't forget to fertilize your strawberry plant once a week.

iii Logical division of ideas

Animals in Zoos

    <u>There are 3 advantages and 3 disadvantages for animals living in zoos.</u> <u>The first advantage of living in a zoo is the animals are kept separated from their natural enemies.</u> The cages protect the animals, thus, they can live without fear of being killed or

maimed. <u>The second advantage</u> is the animals are fed regularly, so they do not have to forage or hunt for food, and they don't go hungry when food is hard to find. <u>The final advantage</u> is the animals' health is well taken care of. All the animals receive medical checks on a regular basis by a veterinarian. As all the animals' needs are catered for in zoos, they live a healthy and happy life. <u>However,</u> <u>despite the 3 advantages, there are 3 disadvantages.</u> <u>The first and most important disadvantage</u> is because they don't have to forage or hunt for their food, they can become board, unhappy, and even aggressive. <u>A second disadvantage</u> is patrons' visits to the zoo can cause some animals to catch human illnesses unless they are protected by walls of glass. <u>In addition,</u> zoo visitors regularly throw human food or scraps to the animals. This inadvertently can kill the animals, or they can become seriously sick. <u>In short,</u> although animals living in zoos can lead a healthy and protected life, the animals can also become bored or perhaps die from human illnesses.

n)   Clauses

Note: some answers may vary.

1. When I graduate from high school, I'll get a job.

2. The *Academic Writing Skills* series, which are good books, help ESL students to write better.

3. I was lonely until Stephen moved to Cambodia.

4. After the game was over, we went shopping.

5. Since I met you in English class, I have improved.

6. I looked like a fool because I didn't think before I spoke.

7. Wait until I call you on Saturday.

8. I love my chemistry teacher, whom I assist as a student aide during my free time

9. Although we were lost, I wasn't afraid.

10. Before you apply to university, be sure to do your research.

o)   Appositives

1. My oldest son, the policeman, will be visiting me next week.

2. Sambat, the author, is very attached to his sister.

3. Apple, a world-wide company, is considering a new iPhone release.

4. An above average student and talented football player Sambat made his father proud.

5. The extremely popular Khmer film Tum Teau was widely criticized for its script.

6. My next door neighbour Mr. Dew is a really good musician.

7. James Dew, Mr. Dew's son, owns a recording studio.

8. Atari, a toy and game manufacturer, came out with Pong, the first video game, in 1972.

9. On Mars, the closest planet to earth, scientists hope to find water.

10. The motorbike a Honda Wave was badly damaged.

Funny Names

The local florist and his wife had a sense of humour when naming their children, <u>three daughters and a son</u>. Their eldest daughter, <u>Lyly</u>, didn't mind being named after a flower. Soken, <u>her best friend</u>, agreed that Lyly was a normal name. By the time their second daughter was born, the florist and his wife, <u>a creative couple</u>, used an unusual name. They named their daughter after the Chrysanthemum, <u>the florist favourite flower</u>. Although it was a difficult name, she didn't really mind it either. Most of her friends just call her Chrissie. By the time daughter number three arrived, her parents decided to be really unique. They named her Delphinium. This youngest daughter, <u>a future biologist</u>, was called Della by her friends. When they had their last child, <u>a boy</u>, they wondered what to call him. They couldn't think of a good blooming plant name for their son. Looking around the floral shop, the florist found something they could use. The unlikely plant <u>a cactus</u> made the florist think of a name more suited to a boy. They bought their new born son, <u>Saguaro</u>, home and showed him to his three sisters. Saguaro, <u>the youngest of the florist's children</u>, turned out to be a handsome young man with no thorns at all.

p) **Complex Sentences**

i **Adverb Clause (subordinating clause)**

Note: some answers may vary.

1. Sambat suggested going to Kirrirom because It was hot and humid in Phnom Penh.

2. When they arrived at Kirrirom, They bought a map of the area's trails.

3. Sengly chose a short trail, whereas Sambat chose a longer more difficult trail.

4. Sengly agreed to go on the more difficult trail as Sambat promised to pay for the hotel room.

5. After they started out on the trail, they left the trail and walked some distance into the forest.

6. When Sengly felt a pain in his arm, he suggested stopping and resting for a while.

7. After Sengly took off his shirt, He found a tick had attached itself to his arm.

8. Both Sambat and Sengly knew ticks carry diseases since they read newspapers and watch TV nature shows.

9. Ticks, including a few in Kirrirom, carry Lyme disease although Sengly wasn't too worried.

10. He removed the tick immediately as he will be less likely to contact the disease.

11. I really enjoyed the concert even though the music was too loud.

12. Mealea needs to learn English, before I teach her academic writing.

13. Stephen played tennis very well while he was very young.

14. Mouy Leng is preparing for the interview now as she wants to get a new job.

15. Vannda will buy the car although he just wants to check with his wife first.

16. William has been working 40 hours a week because there is a big class presentation next week.

17. I usually exercise in the morning before I leave for work at 7.30 am.

18. Sen Kosal didn't have much money although he bought the motorbike.

19. Sen Kosal enjoys going to the movies with his friend Lisa when she visits once a week.

20. During rainy season, since we have a lot of rain, I put the patio furniture in the garage.

ii   Adjective Clause (relative Clauses)

Note: some answers may vary.

1. Sambat, who plays football every day, won the competition.

2. The video game that you lent me had a virus which affected my computer.

3. Where is my English book which was on the desk?

4. Instead of watching TV, I prefer playing computer games, which are more interesting.

5. What was the name of the girl whom you saw on Facebook.

6. The new tennis coach whom none of the players like wants the team to practise more.

7. The school has decided to call a parent meeting that will start at 6 pm tonight.

8. Sambat, whose house is near the park, goes jogging every day.

9. In May, I'm going to Perth, which is where my sister lives.

10. My English teacher, who had an accident, is back in class today.

11. I tried to talk to the girl whose motorbike had run out petrol in front of my house.

12. Where is the attendant whose services we need.

13. Sokleng, who lives on the corner, is a tuk tuk driver.

14. Where is the man who ordered the coffee.

15. The banana which fell behind the couch four days ago is inedible.

16. The tourist whom we met in Siem Reap last week comes from Cambodia.

17. Where is the bottle of orange juice that I bought last night.

18. I borrowed these English books, which are more than 300 pages long, for my assignment.

19. Sokeng, who rarely worries about the cost of things, is a wealthy man.

20. I saw a painting that was painted at Ankor Wat on the wall.

21. She married a man whom she met on the bus.

22. He has written a book in which I have forgotten the name.

23. In 2005, he met Lyly, whom he later married.

24. Dr. Smith is a person whom I don't have much time.

25. We listened to a speech which was interesting, yesterday

26. The students who you just met are in my English class.

27. The chair that I sat on was wet.

28. Khmer New year is a when Khmer people celebrate the new theveda.

29. Stephen tutors ESL students who need help with English writing.

30. Diamonds, are mined in Cambodia, are valuable gems

q)   *Simple, Compound, or Complex*

1	Complex	6	Simple
2	Compound	7	Complex
3	Comples	8	Compound
4	Simple	9	Simple
5	Complex	10	Complex

r)   *Sentence Combining*

1.

Our Fridge

I share a fridge with my flat mate. My side of the fridge is disorganised, grimy, and discoloured. A box of broken eggs sits on the top fridge shelf. Sticks of celery and cold meats share the second fridge shelf with the tomatoes and bread. The celery is wilted, and the cold meats smell, while the bread is stale, and the tomatoes are yucky. Lasagne sits on top of slices of leftover pepperoni pizza on the third fridge shelf. The bottom fridge crisper contains an intriguing variety of food in plastic bags and cardboard boxes from Lucky Burger, KFC, and Taco Bill. A small icky brown pond covers the bottom of the fridge. My flat mate and I are not the same, but we get along ok.

2.

Chetra's Sister

My name is Chetra, and I am 13-years-old. I live in Phnom Penh with my parents and sister, Sopheap. My sister and I go to the same school. Sopheap is a normal girl, however, she likes to tell untrue stories about our family For example, last month, she said our family comes from Australia, and we lived on a beach and rode kangaroos. Of course, the story is untrue and a complete fabrication. All of our family was born in Cambodia, and we have never been to Australia. I wish Sopheap would stop telling embarrassing stories.

s)   *Using Quotes*

1. "Are we there yet?" she asked.

2. The construction engineer said to us, "The building would not collapse."

3. "I'm tired," the boy said, and then drifted off to sleep.

4. "We really should be going now," she said.

5. "Excuse me," he said. "Do you have a light?"

6. "Daddy can I have a banana?" he said.

7. The Prime minister yelled, "We must have peace!"

8. "Sambat said, 'you can go now,'" his friend repeated.

9. The mother said to her friend, "The child simply has a lot of energy."

10. I received "a fail" on my homework because I forgot to write my name on it.

About the Author

The author, Stephen E. Dew, is a veteran of 33 years in the Telecommunication Industry from Australia. He obtained an Associate Diploma in Engineering in 1997 and achieved several units towards a Graduate Certificate in Management by 2004. Having relocated to Perth in 2005, after 5 years in Melbourne writing strategic papers for his business unit, he settled in Bedford and began writing as hobby.

In 2008, he left the Telecommunications sector and travelled SE Asia, where he finally settled in Cambodia. In 2010, he obtained his TESOL qualifications and a Graduate Diploma in Enterprise Applied Management in 2011. He now teaches academic English writing to Khmer ESL students at a well renowned University in Phnom Penh.

In 2014, the author established his AWS ESL Student Academy website for his ESL writing classes and courses, and his AWS Facebook page, which boasts more than 12,000 community members.

Stephen is married and enjoys time with his family, teaching, and writing which are three of his passions. For more information about the author visit Amazon Author Central.

Please note if you enjoyed or learned something from this book, I would appreciate if you could leave a review on Amazon. To leave a review, go to the Amazon author's page, find the English writing exercises book, navigate to the book's reviews, and leave an honest review.

Discover the "Academic Writing Skills" series for ESL students.

  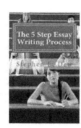 

If you are seeking more information about paragraph writing techniques, English essay writing, the English writing process, or some additional ESL writing grammar exercises, then visit the author's Amazon page. If you wish to follow the authors "Academic Writing Skills" series or academic English writing courses or be informed of future book releases or updates, then register at the Authors website.

Stephen E. Dew
TESOL Instructor and author of the series
"Academic Writing Skills."

This page has been
left blank
intentionally.

CPSIA information can be obtained
at www.ICGtesting.com
Printed in the USA
LVHW051037020723
751362LV00031B/697